EDGAR

PREVIOUS BOOKS BY MALCOLM CARSON

Poetry
Breccia
Rangi Changi
Route Choice
Cleethorpes Comes to Paris
The Where and When
(all published by Shoestring Press)

Also:
Skye Winter

EDGAR

MALCOLM CARSON

Shoestring Press

Printed by imprintdigital
Upton Pyne, Exeter
www.digital.imprint.co.uk

Typesetting and cover design by The Book Typesetters
hello@thebooktypesetters.com
07422 598 168
www.thebooktypesetters.com

Published by Shoestring Press
19 Devonshire Avenue, Beeston, Nottingham, NG9 1BS
(0115) 925 1827
www.shoestringpress.co.uk

First published 2023
© Copyright: Malcolm Carson
© Cover photographs: Caroline Carson

The moral right of the author has been asserted.

ISBN 978-1-915553-21-8

ACKNOWLEDGEMENTS

Thanks are due to the editors of various magazines who have published these poems over the years. The first to appear was 'Edgar goes bait digging' and was published in *Grand Piano* in 1985. Others have been published by *South*, *London Grip* and *Poetry Salzburg Review*. Most have eventually been included in my four Shoestring collections whereas some appear here for the first time.

For Caroline

CONTENTS

Edgar goes bait digging   1

Edgar watches the heron   2

Edgar in Stanwix   3

Edgar sits by the Eden   5

Edgar refuses marriage   6

Edgar is happy   7

Edgar in winter   8

Edgar considers a mortgage   9

Edgar by the Gelt   10

Edgar takes an allotment   11

Edgar tends his cacti   12

Edgar thinks about taking up a sport   13

Edgar visits the Abbey   15

Edgar regards his attire   16

Edgar in love   17

Edgar regards the politicians   18

Edgar at harvest time   19

Edgar and the geese   20

Edgar and his chronicler   21

Edgar in a time of pestilence   22

Edgar revisits the shore   23

EDGAR GOES BAIT DIGGING

'The art of our necessities is strange,
And can make vile things precious.' – King Lear

Tines turn worm casts
in the estuary sand, mudded.
Fingers in half-light grasp

for soft, fat lugs,
broad belted for
coupling head to tail –

slimy exchange of egg,
sperm, across clitella.
Edgar slings another into

the heaving bucket, watches
muddled writhings from his haunches,
considers it necessity

to skewer them
with hooks, the barb
running up their gut.

Lines to be set before
tide's stealthy onrush
up creaks, the riches

of codling, precious inheritance,
in dark anonymous currents:
that's something yet.

1

EDGAR WATCHES THE HERON

I am done with the foul fiend
– Tom haunts the hawthorn
on the windy slope
like antique plastic
on by-pass fence.
            I am here
above the river called Eden
running black as brother's deeds,
father's ignorance, my knowledge.
I watch the heron in the marbled eddies
that catch the moon.
His eye's the thing
which gives a meaning to the rest;
such fastidious engineering
a lethal reed that will wait,
wait for the lazy bask
of salmon, strike.
I need its patience, the breath
of earnest concentration,
need to know the moment
just as the moon torches through
the shattered cloud.

EDGAR IN STANWIX

Traffic lights on Stanwix Bank.
I sup the smell of resin from
bark of logs from Borders hills
stacked high and neat as matches
on juggernauts that strain and lurch
against their brakes in a fog of fumes.
In the Crown I settle to
others' banter, take comfort from
apartness, work on the riddle
of myself amid all this.
Poor Tom, look at stains
on chairs and faces through filter of smoke
grotesqueries of teeth, leers,
see reflected what I imagine is
myself in mirrors above the bar.
Too many of me here. Am I all
the same? Whose meagre crown is this,
on Scotland Road? Do I belong
north or south? I turn to the window
see the cyber café close,
logging off identities
across the ether that settle in
the mind, as real as blood, as ratsbane.
O! do de, do de, do de.
In Tarraby Lane I count the hedge:
holly, alder, maple, beech,
plashed, pleached, layered –where am
I from? Sheep avoid me as does
the pelting moon above the vallum.
Do I hear cavalry's drum on the plain?
Spectres who stripped others of
their souls – unhappy ditto – fashioned
new selves that sit as well as armour.

Should I look in this marsh pool, draw
aside its oily curtain, find
someone looking out beyond
my best, my worst imaginings?
I can pick kingdoms in the bark
of hawthorn, split them, make bigger
on a whim. I can sleep with the holly
against my cheek, suffer cold winds
and persecutions of the sky.
Why then, Tom…Edgar is all one?

EDGAR SITS BY THE EDEN

Look for the kingfisher
see it stitch its silks
above the falls. Wait, wait…
it should come from among the willows.

See the salmon slob
in eddies. Who could end
such memory on the whim
of line's tug and tease?

Will the vole return
to banks where swanky mink
invade the commonwealth
of beasts and willow?

The balsam stinks so sweetly
above the nettles,
and noble thistle, belies
its swelling armoury of seeds.

I mould the river
to my days, choose
a runnel of debate,
follow debris's swift demise.

Best like this, for too much
cogitation draws me down
to depths where sorrow lies.
I will bear free and patient thoughts.

EDGAR REFUSES MARRIAGE

In Nahum Tate's 1681 reworking of *King Lear*, he has Edgar
marry Cordelia in order to effect a happy ending.

Why should he think to tear her from her father's
arms who looks in vain for mist on looking-glass?
How pluck her from that happy prison where
they would have laughed at lesser beings gad
round fortune's hooves like angry clegs? Does he think
we suffer less when happiness contrives
to dull our senses to the tempest in our hearts?

Ninny! Does he suppose I'll settle for
a salvaged fate, pretend I never was
on that heath, Poor Tom, was never called by Frateretto
or saw my father blinded by blind judgement's storm?
I'll not accept the solace of a truth
ignored for then would Edgar be abused,
his marriage bed be racked with barbs and blisters,
his coupling demented with the cries of bride
and groom for their gross betrayal.

I'll have none of it. Instead I'll clip the box
tend lavender, bruise the thyme on broken paths,
watch the heron, do such unrelated
things that never will amount to much,
that never will feed an ending to the fatuous crowd.

EDGAR IS HAPPY

I am distracted from dark thoughts,
join in delight, despite myself,
at small birds that dink to my feeder.
Such a flutter of the soul.
Brazen chaffinch drops offerings
to his happy other, skirrs
to the hedge. Stately pigeon
lumps across the lawn
scouring for orts.
Woodpecker stabs its presence.
I could pick a diamond blade of grass to gaze on,
but am happy as I am for now.
I know that Frateretto may call
and Tom follow, that the foul fiend
lurks, but still this day at least
includes me in the parliament
of things glorious.

EDGAR IN WINTER

It is the trees above all
veining the grey
where geese come in
haunting the dark
afternoon, when sky
pulls back with
the slow lap of Solway
seeping round pocks
of grass and thrift
where marsh cows
threaten with their looks
and you want to get past
before they guess your fear
and the urgent breath frosts
with your heart.

EDGAR CONSIDERS A MORTGAGE

They lay around me those
who I have loved, even
the one who cashed in my trust
for private gain. Pledged to death

their mortgage now is paid.
What need for me to guess
the span of years in which
I have a right to my own soul?

Capital might be gained,
some comfort in supposing
I have a tenure on my life
that will allow the heart

to heal, repair the misery
that I bear, and with the wisdom
of some quiet years become
at peace with poor Tom.

Yet there's no guessing at events
or how our pretty thoughts
may still prove treasonous.
Tides kiss the walls

and seasons confute their rote.
I look in vain for idle things
to dandle in my mind, decide
to pocket what I know.

EDGAR BY THE GELT

It's wild today,
thrashes into groins that
turn its dissent
downstream.
Boulders grumble
beneath breakers,
white water
where once I soaked,
still, cold in the marrow
of summer night.
It troubles me this flux
of moods, watching.
My fingers green
with slime on ash.
Fungi burst through
the bark of fallen birch.
No chance of settling,
for nothing lasts
yet all's the same.
The squirrel is alert
to simple duties
and its necessary play.
I should be happy,
for this commonwealth
where I have a part,
can watch and maunder,
be particular at will.
The politics of buzzard,
goldcrest, salmon, vole,
will not ensnare me.

EDGAR TAKES AN ALLOTMENT

My patch for a time, this, allotted.
I will clear it of persistent menace –
twitch, dock and neighbouring nettle,
ground elder that Romans brought for salad.
I will pick each snip of broken root
for from neglect more vexation grows.
I'll light a fire that signals my intent,
smoulders with the efforts of my weeding,
comforts as I crouch on aching thighs
picking among unruly soil.
I have a palisade of corrugated iron
and stakes, know my estate's dimensions
as neighbours know theirs. My shed
is where I will prepare for proper husbandry,
the planting of sound stock
that will reward with crops
of known provenance.
Cinders, soot, my vigilance
will deter marauders that would infect
the core of all that's good.

EDGAR TENDS HIS CACTI

Aliens these in our ferny land:
a tuft of cushion and a spine

that pinions flies to desiccate,
skin glossy to the sun's scrutiny,

folds for economy,
a seeming stasis. Slow

a bloom grows, and in a day
is gone, a berry as a wound.

I stand over them, watch
for impossible movement,

my little kingdom
of towers, cathedrals,

squat dwellings, and those
that skulk as pebbles.

Too much love, too little,
and all's undone, for then

they bloat beyond their compass
or ignored in the gazebo

shrivel and expire.
Should I forget my function

weeds will purloin the light,
usurp my proud dominion.

EDGAR THINKS ABOUT TAKING UP A SPORT

I wonder should I take a sport
as partner in my contemplations
for then would grief be as if shared
through strong exertion, sweat.

No chance of falling by the way
should weariness overwhelm me
for I could call on my resources,
strong in mind and sinew.

Too much debate on haunches' gloom
enfeebles me, I'm sure, lets cramps,
foul thoughts thicken in the blood
and enemies gain strength.

Yet what to follow? For I have
watched cricket, tennis, other games
where teams plot and counter,
use subterfuge and undermine

authority. No harm in that
of itself where the law's corrupt,
but here's too close to what
I know of family and kings.

So, no team for me, no bonds
that would suffocate or then be found
too slight when loyalty
is looked for and not received.

The fell's the place where I will range
free from all constraint
but body's limitations, where
when the foul fiend calls

I'll outrun him, fleet of foot, through
oily marsh and bracken trods,
leave scant prints between webbed reeds
where bog cotton glows.

He'll not find me, bewildered by
my new found strength:
Edgar resilient on the moor,
defiant as the crags he leaps.

EDGAR VISITS THE ABBEY

Their proffered plan in hand, I navigate
the aisles. Tom's devils are here yet I must resist,
turn from gargoyles' mocking gawp, think of such things
as merely blocks of stone invested in
by mason's craft, reaching out for meaning,
with chisel, trowel, set-square, compass: trades
where the spirit resides, happy in itself.

Yet the choir haunts, its gothic stalls seem
in judgement of our pleasant vices, prepare
to plague us. Misericords offer scant
compassion, and organ pipes will bellow the fiend within.

I pass the painted tableau of another's passion,
– too much to bear – and find my way past lids
of graves and effigies of stately dames,
smoothed from prurient hands, ignore the crypt
that beckons, too dark too soon. Instead
I seek lofted thoughts where light defies the gloom;
I will adopt 'clerestory' for in that word
lies hope when Tom is in ill thoughts again.

Enough for now. I head towards the slype
and drop a coin in a collection box.
A payment for a clarity of sorts.

EDGAR REGARDS HIS ATTIRE

Little help against the wind and rain
and calls from Tom. The clothes I have
show stains of murderous events,
conspiracies and blind jealousy's child.
Burrs cling to the troubled heart,
Robin-run-the-hedge teases
the skin to scratch away where nothing is,
sets up a cause of intemperate heat.
My legs bear evidence of brashing's scores
just like the flail of father's words
or brother's calumnies which breeches
cannot forefend.

EDGAR IN LOVE

I think I am in love, or how I imagine
that state to be since I have only

my views of others and how they behave,
supposedly enamoured.

Yet I've seen devotion cloud their minds,
ambition of the noblest kind befogged.

I also know that what goes for love
sometimes is no more than coupling for

dishonour's sake. So what makes me so sure,
experience being so jaundiced, that my devotion

is any different? A prey to hypocrisy?
I can't be certain and can only hope

that she knows not of my love, cares not,
thereby ensuring a purity of spirit.

Even as I say it though, I realise
the pathos of such nonsense.

No, forget it. I am not in love,
no *Porte Étroite* for me.

EDGAR REGARDS THE POLITICIANS

I have seen them peeking out of holes, watching
if the land is clear before they utter
reckless things, draw back, and let the caterwauling
crowd take up their cry. Only then
from burrows do they emerge, seeming to
reflect the popular will with mock reluctance,
forced to heed 'the common good'. They leer
and fawn and seem offended by obstructions
from dissenters, impeders of the people's will.
Behind the scenes, they skulk in improbable liaisons
which will unravel upon the hour when chance's
easy option allows for seeing off
a rival's threat. (Those sisters know a thing
or two, as does my brother whom they crave.
Such concupiscence!) Yet still I hope that in
their moil they either tire or get found out
and perish by each other's hand. Or yet
will nature have vengeance? Too much to hope? Perhaps,
but what else if there's to be a rebalancing
of order after the dark hours of a disordered world?

EDGAR AT HARVEST TIME

I assume a role by the gate,
leaning in my fustian, watching
with inconsequence the gleaners
among the stubble, the castled stooks,
or where the trailer leaked
its precious load. Meagre allowances
for backs near-broken from bearing
sacks up ladders that creaked
as much as bones. Small birds
move in behind their shuffle
– all is safely gathered in.
There will be celebrations,
a reckoning of good process,
loyalty, and so with them
I'll throw off morbidity,
ignore life's disproportion until
such time as I can deal justly.

EDGAR AND THE GEESE

How I love their call
that reaches into
my darkest time.
I may be engrossed
in such important things,
yet must draw
apart and gaze into
the winter sky,
seek out their echelon
and soar toward them.
They might settle,
if I'm in luck,
on these sodden fields
where grass invites
replenishment,
or else pass over to
Solway's reaches
where bitter winds
and cruel skies seem
as nothing at journey's end.
I will take comfort
for my afflictions,
when the flight of geese
enriches so.

EDGAR AND HIS CHRONICLER

Who are you who places me
in such odd circumstance,
in times incongruous to mine,
allows me to speak in language
I couldn't know? And then you dare
to fancy how I might feel
in time's disjuncture,
let alone when family turns upon itself.
Still, I'll not spin round on chance
of catching you spying behind
the transept column, or playing
wildfowler on Solway's flats,
for then would my adventures cease,
and I'd be folded back
into the pages of a play,
my story that of a grieving son,
a brother wronged, who,
though still victorious,
is just another in
a dramatis personae. Much better
to let you do as you will,
though the time may come
when I'll chide you
for too much liberty.
So, be careful how you tread,
whoever you are.

EDGAR IN A TIME OF PESTILENCE

I watch the bat at dusk,
chauve souris, sweeping

up the midges that cloud
my hair. All's obscure,

oscura, as though the laurels,
yews, the graveyard trees,

speak of matters I know
too well when the mind's diseased.

Amid it all, the bat
sounds out impediments,

and in a tilt of wing
or thought dips away.

Would we had loved its cleverness
before darkness induced in us

such arrogance, a carapace
of intelligence where we'd no thought

to look beyond ourselves.
And now the foul fiend

runs amok. Meantime
my little pipistrelle

dances in the dark,
l'ombrage, crepusculum.

EDGAR REVISITS THE SHORE

It was here, I remember,
I dug for bait. The tide

out beyond the creeks,
castles made by worms

giving away their safety
to probing forks.

I look across to pools
where the diggers were,

to breakwaters reaching
out to a rib of tide,

striations where curlew
probe, and waders

are set up by errant dog,
perfect in flighted alarm.

Where now 'Tom'?
On seeing this again,

do I need him still, or
will he persist despite

best efforts to put behind
the time upon the heath?

Who's to know? As light
seeps with the tide,

my shadow lengthens
across the sand, stretching

with the minute until
it will extinguish in the gloom.

Yet I am glad I came,
for only by gazing at

the darkest hour, can Edgar
be himself. *Ripeness is all.*